D0521777

Draw and Color
Pets

Learn to draw and color 23 favorite animals, step by easy step, shape by simple shape!

Illustrated by Peter Mueller

Walter Foster®

Getting Started

When you **look** closely at the **drawings** in this book, you'll notice that they're made up of basic shapes, such as circles, triangles, and rectangles. To draw all your favorite animal friends, just start with simple shapes as you see here. It's easy and fun!

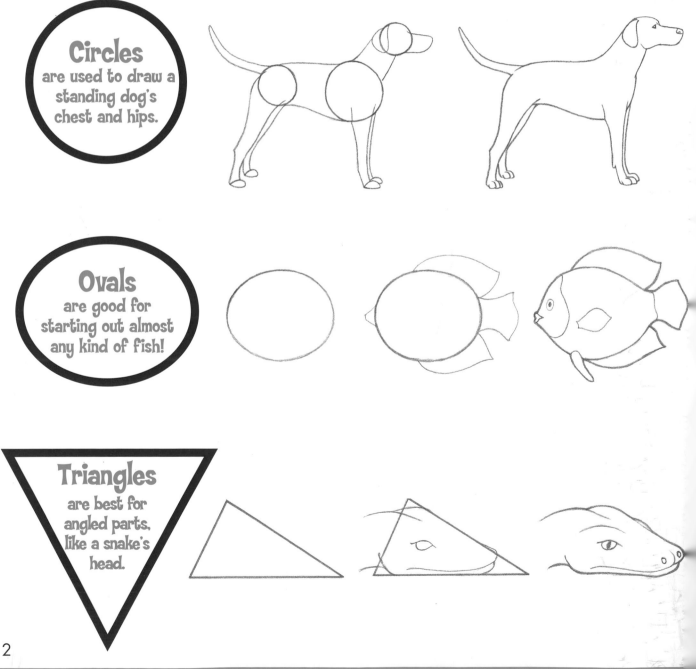

Circles are used to draw a standing dog's chest and hips.

Ovals are good for starting out almost any kind of fish!

Triangles are best for angled parts, like a snake's head.

Coloring Tips

There's more than one way to bring your **pet pals** to life on paper—you can use crayons, markers, or colored pencils. Just be sure you have plenty of natural colors—black, brown, gray, and white, plus yellow, orange, and red.

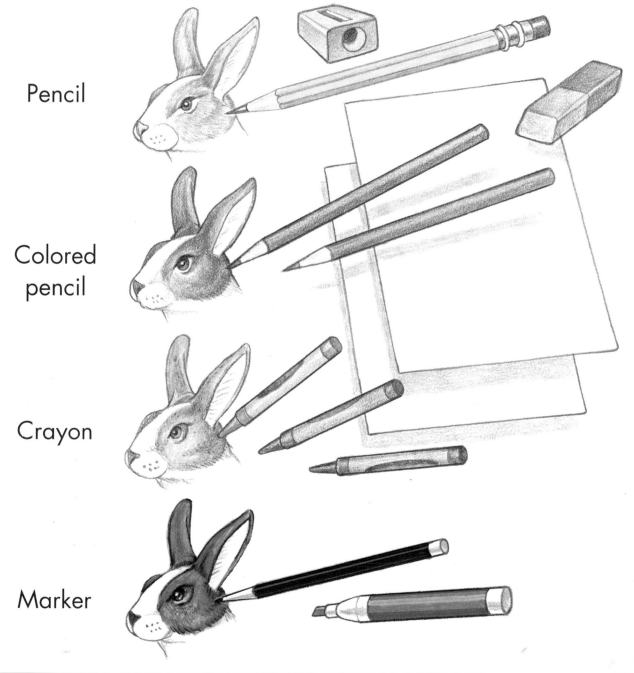

Pencil

Colored pencil

Crayon

Marker

Puppy

This **lovable** Lab is still a youngster, so it has a **chubby** body. Begin with an oval for the tummy and a circle for the head.

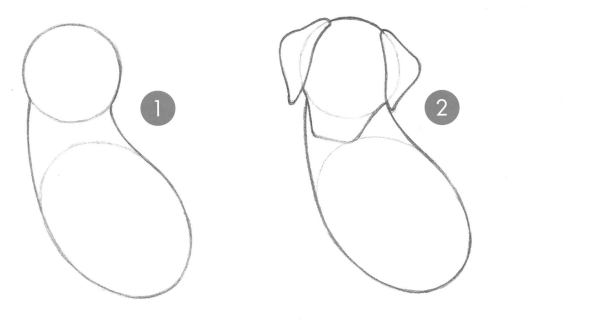

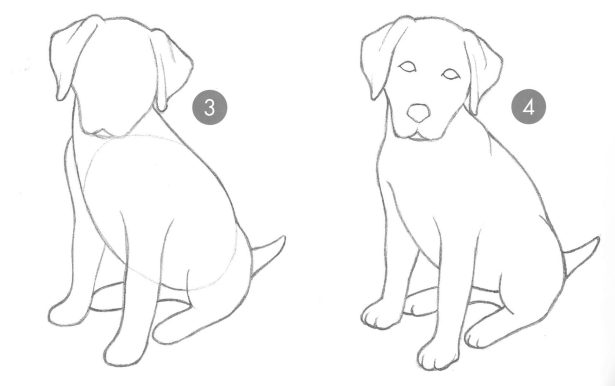

★ ★ ★ ★ ★ ★ ★ ★ ★ ★ ★ ★ ★ ★ ★ ★ ★ ★

5

fun fact

Even puppies who are "free to a good home" need care and upkeep—and that takes cash. So how much can you expect to spend on that doggie in the window? Get out your piggy bank! On average, it costs $6400 to raise one medium-sized dog from a puppy to the age of 11.

6

Kitten

This tiny **tabby** has a **fluffy** body and short, thick legs.
Its round eyes and triangular ears look huge on its little furry frame!

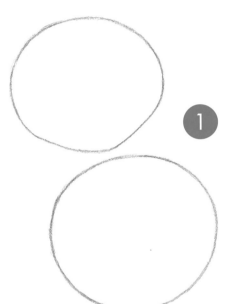

fun fact

Cats have excellent hearing and very flexible ears! They have 30 outer-ear muscles, which can rotate each ear a full 180 degrees. So felines can hear in all directions without moving their heads, which helps them pinpoint where sounds are coming from.

Macaw

Use an oval to draw this **colorful**, exotic **parrot's** body.
The bird's long feathers come to a point—so does its sharp, curved beak!

Most people know that a macaw's beak is powerful—it's so strong that it can easily crush a Brazil nut! But what's less well known is that a macaw also use its dry, scaly tongue as a tool. A bone inside the tongue helps the bird break open and eat food.

Bunny

This **Lop-eared** rabbit's body is **round**, but it isn't a perfect circle. Its long ears droop down, but its short tail swoops up!

fun fact

It's not unusual for caretakers to discover their pet bunnies fast asleep. After all, rabbits are nocturnal, which means they're active at night, so they sleep during the day. And, on average, rabbits take 16 naps per day to get in a full 8 hours of sleep!

Frog

It isn't easy being **green!** This **amphibian** has a few unusual features, like legs that fold and eyes that sit on top of its head!

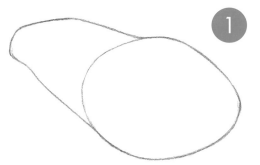

1

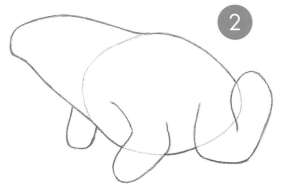

2

3

4

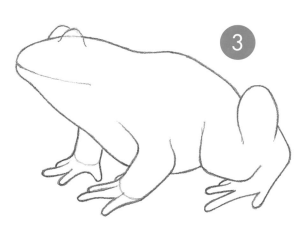

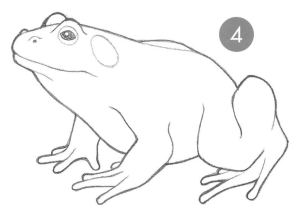

5

fun fact

There are a few species of frogs that can thaw out and return to life after being frozen. But don't try this at home! Since these frogs account for only a few of the 2600 known frog species, you don't want to experiment on your hip-hopper!

Mouse

This **little** mammal has tiny **rodent** features: small, round eyes; a tiny pink nose; a long, thin tail; and itty, bitty toenails!

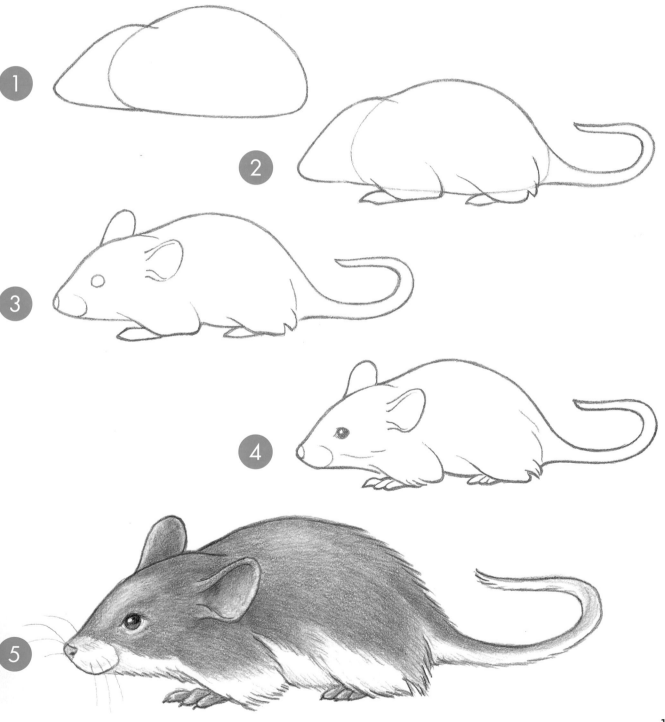

1

2

3

4

5

Ferret

With its **slim** body and small head, the ferret looks similar to a **cat!** But its rounded ears and masked markings distinguish it from most pets.

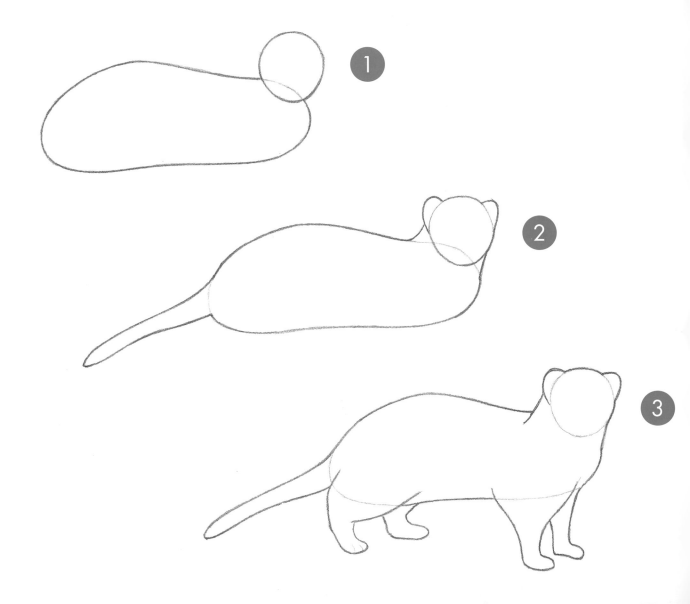

1

2

3

fun fact

Ferrets have been domesticated for even longer than cats have. Yet the approximately 8 million domestic ferrets in the United States aren't officially recognized as pets by any state government, and it's illegal to own these furry friends in the state of California!

Horse

Start this horse on the right **track** by drawing the **main** shapes: two circles for the hips and chest. Then trot along to the other parts!

fun fact

Horses don't lay eggs or raise tadpoles, but they do reproduce frogs. Confused? The soft underside of a horse's hoof is called a "frog." The frog sheds every time there is new growth, which happens several times each year.

Betta

fighting fish

Male Japanese fighting fish are known for their large, colorful fins, which they proudly display when they meet another male fish!

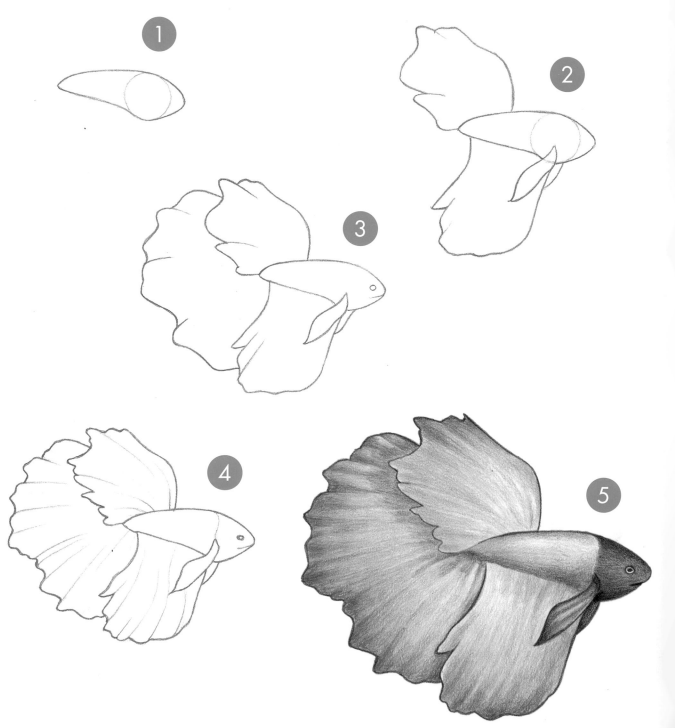

Cockatiel

The cockatiel's **crown** of feathers **stands up** when the bird is excited, but it lies flat and curls at the end when the bird is calm.

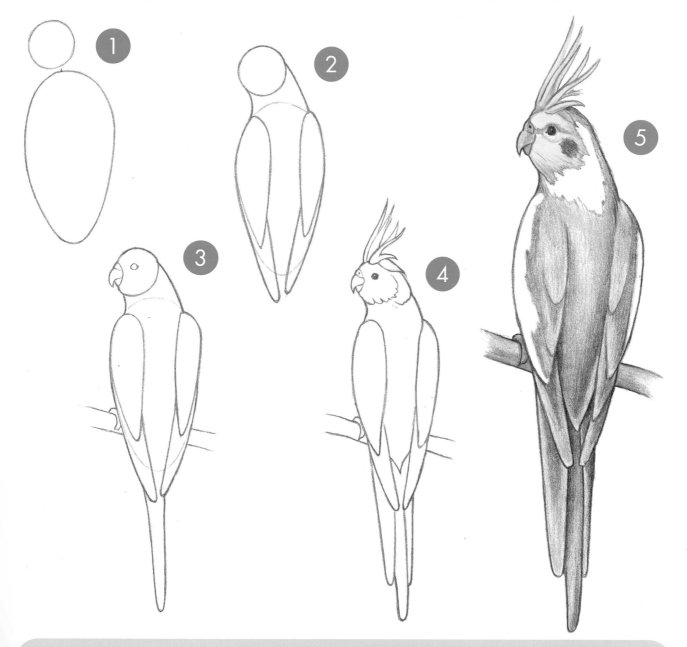

fun fact

Because it's a social bird, your cockatiel might enjoy having a pet of its own! Experts say canaries make good pets for cockatiels. But don't expect your 'tiel to take care of the canary's feeding and cleanup; those will be your responsibilities!

Tropical Fish

Why stop at one **fish** when you can draw a whole aquarium? Fill the water with Yellow Tangs, Moorish Idols, Blowfish, and more!

21

Dog

A **Rottweiler** has a thick, stocky body and a **big** head. Draw this powerful dog with strong legs, a square jaw, and a straight back.

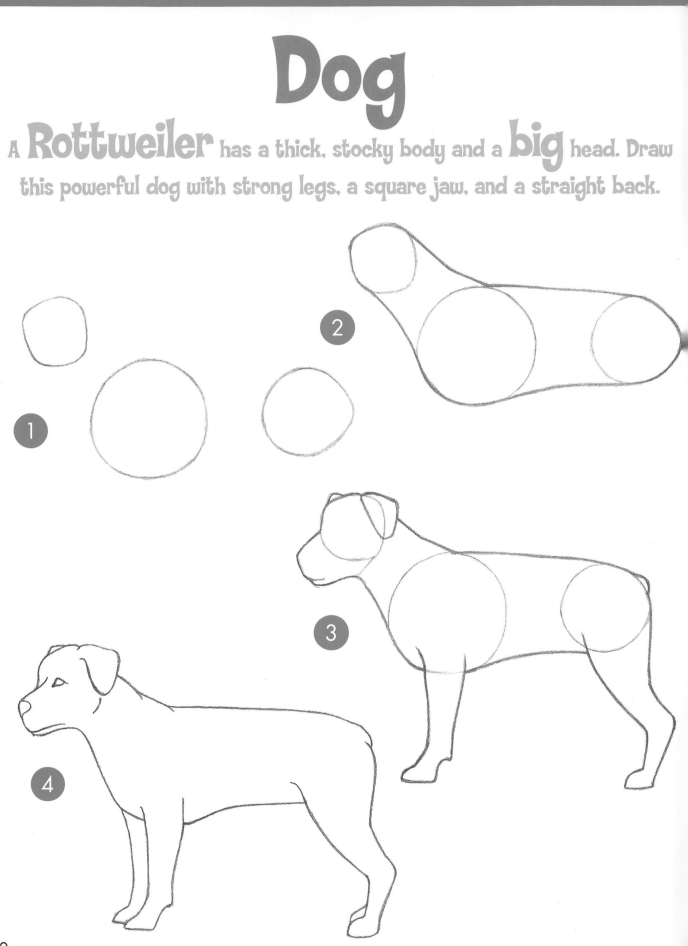

22

fun fact

Many people incorrectly believe that the Canary Islands, located in Spain, were named after the bird. Actually, the islands were named after the Latin *Canariae insulae*, where "Canariae" refers to a large breed of dogs from Roman times. So the islands' name really means "Isle of Dogs"!

Iguana

When you draw this **scaly**, sun-loving **reptile**, be sure to make its tail longer than its head and body combined!

fun fact

Iguanas are a favorite pet in the United States, but they're a favorite meal in Central America! Iguana dishes are so common there that these reptiles are sometimes referred to as *gallina del palo,* or "chicken of the tree"!

Short-Haired Cat

It's easy to **spot** this **feline's** shape because of its short coat! Start drawing this regal Bengal's body with a tall bean shape.

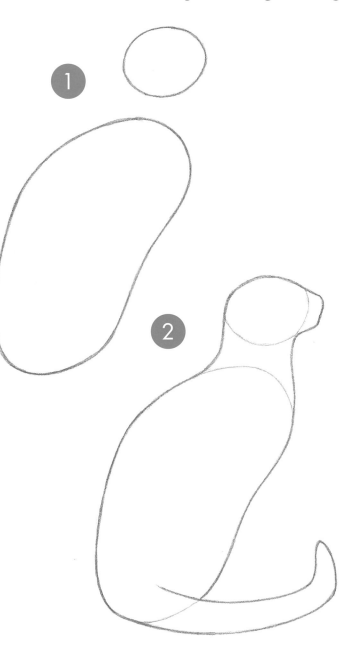

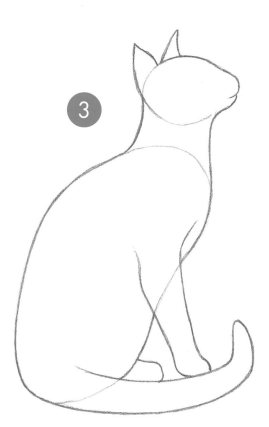

fun fact

Do you see a resemblance between your kitty and the big cats at the zoo? It may be because your house cat is part wild cat. The first house cats—domesticated more than 4000 years ago—were descendants of African and European wild cats!

Parakeets

This **pair** of parakeets starts out with **similar** shapes, but the birds aren't identical. Look for the differences as you draw.

Goldfish

Like a game of **Go Fish**, drawing this goldfish is as simple as can be! Begin with an egg shape for the body, and then add the flowing fins!

1

2

3

4

5

fun fact

The most common name for pet goldfish in the United States is "Jaws." But Jaws isn't likely to respond to its name—or even remember it. The average memory span of a goldfish is only 3 seconds!

Pot-Bellied Pig

"Porkers" like this one love to pig out, so it's no surprise that this swine's most recognizable feature is its big round belly.

1

2

3

fun fact

With their love for both slop and mud, pigs have gained a reputation for being lazy. But pigs are actually capable of great bursts of energy. At top speed, they can run a full mile in only 7.5 minutes—that's 8 miles per hour!

Snake

S-s-s-start with two oval shapes to **snake** yourself into position to draw this slithery coiled Python.

32

Hermit Crab

Like all **hermits,** this crab prefers to be **alone.** And there's no better place to retreat from the world than inside a shell!

1

2

3

4

5

fun fact

Hermit crabs aren't terribly friendly about sharing their space with others. If two of these crabs encounter one another, watch the claws fly: The hermits will battle it out until one falls out of its shell.

Pony

Ponies are **shorter** than horses, but they're usually stronger as well! Draw this pet with a thick body and muscular legs.

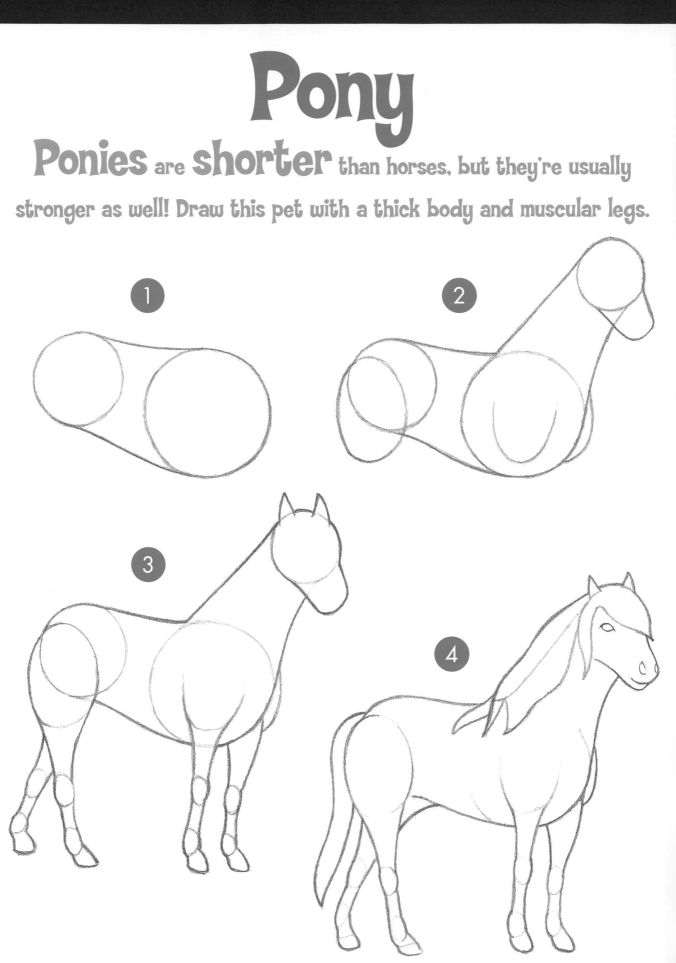

fun fact

In the short time the Pony Express operated—from 1860 to 1861—the mail service employed nearly 400 animals and 100 riders. But don't let the name "Pony Express" fool you; the company never hired a single pony—they preferred Mustang and Morgan horses!

Tarantula

An **Arachnid** is a different kind of "**furry**" friend! This spider has eight shaggy legs and two shorter "arms" in front of its body.

1

2

4

3

5

Tarantulas are the only spiders that aren't able to spin webs strong enough to support their own weight.

Tortoise

This **shell-back** moves **slowly** because it takes its home wherever it goes! Its four thick, strong legs have to work hard.

Long-Haired Cat

Is there a **body** under all that **fluff?** Of course! But to draw a purr-fect Persian portrait, just draw the shapes that you can see!

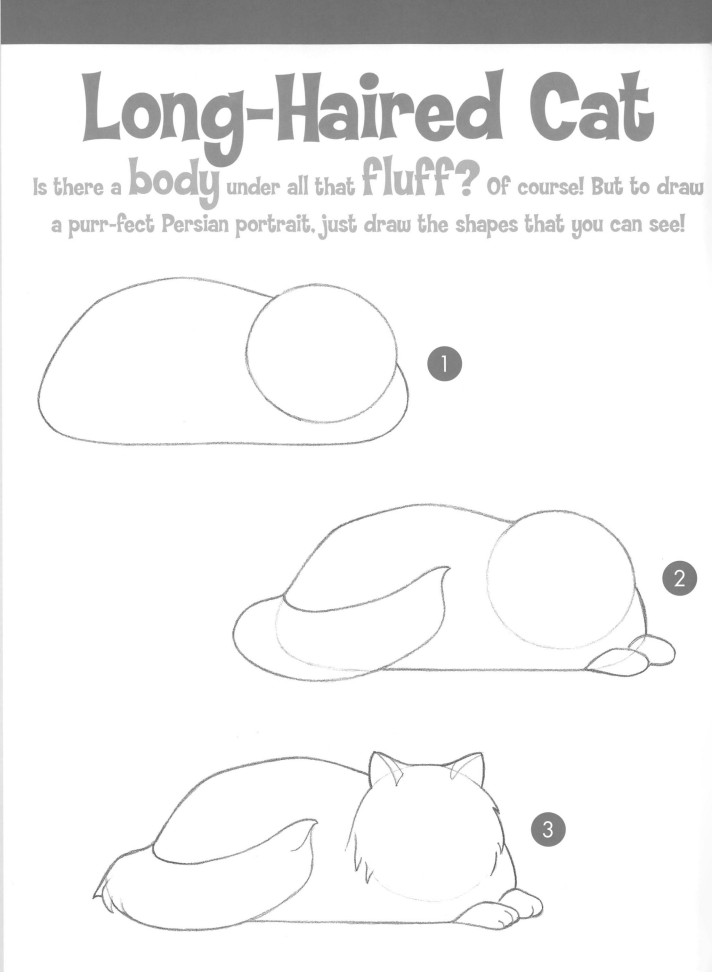

fun fact

The "color point" pattern of cats like the one above is determined by heat! Color-point kittens are born light-colored because they are warm inside their mothers. After birth, the cool temperature areas (or points) of the cat darken.

Guinea Pig

This little **cowlicked furball** is more closely related to a mouse than to a pig. It may be the only pet with permanent "bedhead"!